IT'S TIME TO MAKE A
CHANGE

With Hope & Joy,

Shari

IT'S TIME TO MAKE A
CHANGE

30 Days to Renew Your
Mind, Heart and Soul

Shani E. McIlwain

purposely
created
PUBLISHING

It's Time To Make a Change
Copyright © 2016 Shani E. McIlwain

Published by: Purposely Created Publishing Group™

Printed in the United States of America

ISBN-13 (ebook): 978-1-942838-89-0
ISBN-13 (paperback): 978-1-942838-88-3

table of contents

acknowledgements

To my superstars, Roderick, Raianna, Michayla, and Elisia, I didn't even know what unconditional love meant until I had each of you. I pray that each of you finds your purpose on earth that brings you great joy. I hope that you smile often, feel the Son shine on you every day, and know always that you are loved.

Moses "Mac" Davis, words simply cannot express how much you mean to me. I am grateful that my mother was able to have those years with you. I thank you for loving my children and me as you do. I love you always.

My husband, Michael, every time I go into writing a book and starting a project, you support me in ways that I often take for granted. I would not be able to be the person I am without your support. I thank you for your love and pray that the Lord continues to bless this union. I hope we continue to run unashamedly to God, who makes everything perfect for us.

Tieshena Davis, my publisher, my mentor, my coach, and my friend, and her company Purposely Created Publishing Group— thank you for every ounce of wisdom you pour into me each day. I am so overjoyed by the opportunity you have given me. I cannot wait to change generations with you, and I am excited about our future! You rock, girl! You are the best!

introduction

Submission Begins with C.H.A.N.G.E.

Loss is God's biggest attention getter. Many of us struggle with a loss, wandering in a feeling of hopelessness, uncertain of which way to turn. My first memory of losing something was at the age of ten when a fire destroyed my home. I learned at that young age that possessions are only temporary. Years later, I would go on to lose relationships that I deeply cared about, each loss becoming greater and serving as another opportunity to grow closer to God. Unfortunately, I boldly ignored them all. By the time I was thirty, I was divorced with two children, from two different men, struggling to find myself. I even lost my mother to cancer and still didn't answer the wakeup call.

In 2009, I had twins, and forty-nine days later one passed away. You would have thought I was ready to really start listening to God's voice, and for a while I did. I knew that I couldn't get past this loss on my own. My friends wouldn't be able to help me, and drinking a vodka and cranberry juice every day just to go to sleep wouldn't help either. I knew losing a child who was only six weeks old just might have me at the end of a cliff ready to jump. Mothers aren't supposed to bury their children. Mothers are supposed to take care of them.

After the mourning, guilt quickly followed. I wondered if I had been so disobedient that God would punish me in the worst way. At least I didn't blame God for losing Alexia. But I did blame myself. I was tired of being tired, and it was time to really take heed of God's plan and direction for my life.

For many of us, submission is a dirty word. But, according to Webster's, submission is *"the action or fact of accepting or yielding to a superior force or to the will or authority of another person."*

Submitting to God is simply a choice, the understanding that the life we live is not ours. 1 Chronicles 7:14 NLT says, *"Then if my people who are called by my name will humble themselves and pray and seek my face and turn from their wicked ways, I will hear from heaven and will forgive their sins and restore their land."*

In order to submit to God, you have to first humble yourself. I spent years being too prideful and coming up with my own version of religion. I am sure you have heard people say that they are a "work in progress." Well, I was a work in progress, too. But the key word in that statement is "work," and I had to be honest with myself: I wasn't really *working* at progress. I loved sinning. And because of this, I found myself further and further from God's voice.

After Alexia passed, I went back to church. Before that, I had church-hopped for years and didn't have a church to call home. My husband felt a loyalty to his childhood church, and I did feel a sense of gratitude to this place because we had had Alexia's funeral there. So, in the summer of 2009, we started to attend services there every Sunday. By October, I had become an active member. Then, I became a super member. I was saying yes to every ministry, even though I was still drinking every night to sleep, which wasn't helping. I was also functioning off less than three hours of sleep each night. I was not submitting to God; I was just doing busy work, and I was emotionally damaged. Years of loss, pain, and regret continued to eat away at my core. I held on to years of resentment and hurt that I wasn't speaking life to, but rather bitterness and condemnation. My humor was sarcastic, and it camouflaged my true feelings. I was going to church every Sunday, but I wasn't getting any better.

My problem was that I had relationship and religion completely wrong. Religion doesn't make people submit to God; relationship does. Having a close personal relationship with Christ is the only way to fully submit to Him. Religion is full of laws and rituals that are necessary but often hard to live up to. God knew that it was hard for us to follow rules. He sent His son to die on the cross so we could have life and have it more abundantly. (John 10:10) An abundant life is filled with success in every aspect of your life, including family, marriage, business, finances, career, and health. It doesn't matter what it is, God has a plan for it. It doesn't matter how small or insignificant you may think it is; scripture says that the Lord will perfect whatever concerns you. (Psalms 138:8). He is waiting with open arms for you to lay it all before Him, and He will guide you through each decision you make.

It took loss after loss and problem after problem to realize that I had not fully submitted to Christ. I hadn't been able to because I didn't completely trust Him. How crazy is that? I believed He was the author of my life, but I couldn't give Him everything. I couldn't let him control everything. I was simply not willing to give up control. I needed to control everything. Yet all my decisions that didn't include God ended in failure.

When my place of employment for nearly twenty years went bankrupt, I was left with no severance, no warning, nothing. I was already late on my rent and a pile of other bills. At that moment, I realized I had put too much into everything except GOD! I trusted my job, no Jesus, to provide all of my needs. But God merely gives us jobs as a resource with which to take care of our families and ourselves. I had relied on the resource instead of the SOURCE.

Looking back, I realize that losing my job was the best thing that had ever happened to me, because it was during this loss that I found Jesus. I knew of Jesus, but I didn't *know* Him. Fortunately, it was a breath of fresh air getting to know Him as my friend, my mediator, my protector, and my source. I may not have known how the rent would get paid or how anything else would work out. But during those unknown times, I submitted completely.

Submission is not a sign of weakness but of strength. Submission is part of trusting God. When we allow God to take control of our lives, our plans, our thoughts, scripture tells us that He will do exceedingly and abundantly more than we can ever expect. But in order to submit, you have to change, which first starts with the way you think. You must realize that you are not in control. I learned this during many sleepless nights. I learned that I couldn't change the fact that I didn't have a job, or that I was applying to jobs that didn't respond. I couldn't change that I had lost a child, but what I could change was my mind. The Creator gives us free will in everything we do, and changing your perspective will help you to activate your faith for success.

Over the next thirty days, we will renew our minds and habits to become more accepting of CHANGE and to define or redefine our purpose. It will be challenging but rewarding. Let's get started.

Peace & Joy in Christ,

Shani

We need to be committed to the **Chief Cornerstone** of our lives. His love calms us, His care comforts us and His sovereignty controls every aspect of our lives.

"The secret of change is to focus all of your energy, not on fighting the old, but on building the new."
- Socrates

DAY 1

Commit to Following Jesus

Matthew 4:19
*"Then He said to them, 'Follow Me,
and I will make you fishers of men.'"*

Being a follower of Christ means aligning your life with His will. Too often we give up on that which seems hard, but God never promised us an easy life. When we stay committed to His word, we can handle any and all challenges that come our way.

Think about what you are doing with your daily commitments to yourself, your relationships, and your obligations.

Do you follow through with things?

Do you break commitments?

Do you cancel plans? If so, why?

It's Time to Make a Change

If you can't commit to God first, all the secondary things in your life will be out of alignment and out of sync.

So ask yourself: How often to you set aside time with God in prayer and study?

Do you start off strong and then wander off, making other things priorities?

Day 1

Today's C.H.A.N.G.E. Action:

"I will make my commitment to Christ the most important thing in my life."

_____

_____

_____

_____

_____

_____

_____

_____

_____

_____

Reflection

_____

_____

_____

_____

_____

_____

_____

_____

_____

_____

_____

_____

_____

DAY 2

He Cares About ME

Psalms 138:8a
"The Lord will perfect that which concerns me"

Do you know how mighty and powerful God is, the God of the universe who can control all things and truly cares about everything? At times, it is hard to wrap our heads around this, but it's so true. We think about the big things like our health, and our finances, and our marriages. But, if we break down each of those aspects of our lives, we find it always applies.

Take for instance our marriages and relationships. Yes, God wants us to have a loving and fulfilling marriage that puts Him first. But he also cares about the small things, like date night.

Rather than complaining that you aren't getting any alone time for a date night, take your concern to God in prayer. If it concerns you, it concerns Him also.

Day 2

Today's C.H.A.N.G.E. Action:

Share your smallest concerns with God, even something you think is a waste of time bringing up. Talk to Him about it, and remember that He perfects everything.

_____

_____

_____

_____

_____

_____

_____

_____

_____

_____

Reflection

_____

_____

_____

_____

_____

_____

_____

_____

_____

_____

_____

_____

_____

DAY 3

Communion with God

2 Corinthians 13:14
"The grace of the Lord Jesus Christ, and the love of God,
and the fellowship of the Holy Spirit, be with you all."

Communion with God is simply fellowship. It is spending time with Him. My days begin with conversation with Christ. I literally set my alarm thirty minutes earlier just so I can snooze for ten minutes and spend the next twenty minutes with my friend. When I don't do that, the day seems backwards, and I feel so lost. It's like not getting coffee before checking your work email. DISASTROUS!

The thing is I enjoy my quiet time with God. Do not let the busyness of something as insignificant as a to-do-list keep you from your alone time. God's thinks your alone time with Him is most important.

Day 3

Focus on your conversations with Christ. Make Him a priority. Set aside moments in which you allow His presence to settle. And just say, "Ahh."

_____

_____

_____

_____

_____

_____

_____

_____

_____

_____

Reflection

_____

_____

_____

_____

_____

_____

_____

_____

_____

_____

_____

_____

DAY 4

God is in Control of Your Life

Proverbs 16:9
"The heart of man plans his way, but the Lord establishes his steps."

When I was in my teens, I had big dreams and even bigger plans. I was going to be a well-paid, no nonsense lawyer who wouldn't get married or have kids. But when I found out that law school was an eight-year program, I thought well, maybe I will be a high school history teacher but a really cool one. I would make history exciting and interact with the kids, but I still wouldn't have any kids, let alone get married. No way! Not me. I am sure most of my high school friends thought the same thing about me, because when I returned for my ten-year reunion, they were so shocked to find out I had two kids and was divorced. I never became a lawyer or a high school history teacher, either. In fact, I had my first son unmarried.

It's Time to Make a Change

When that relationship ended, I thought being a single parent wasn't part of my plan. Deep down I felt ashamed. And that shame set in motion a domino effect of bad decisions. I married prematurely, had another child, divorced a year later, and then spent years searching not just for my plans, but also my purpose, even searching to be saved. By the time I was in my thirties, I said, "Well, society thinks I am an okay person. I may have not done everything by the book, but I was truly still searching for something greater. Mike and I weren't married, and I had three more babies within a year of each other. And when Alexia passed at forty-nine days old, we were devastated.

Immediately, I ran to a church so I could find a way to cope with this loss. I knew Jesus, but only in trouble. When I was in trouble, Jesus was my best friend. He was my handy tissue box whenever I couldn't stop the tears. And once He dried my eyes, I would be back doing my own thing, setting my own plans. But this time was different. This loss, this tragedy, I couldn't handle alone. I was tired of holding on to different versions of what the truth was. As I began to heal and grow in the word of God, everything around me grew with it. On the last day of that same year, Mike and I were married.

God has a way of orchestrating your plans to eventually fit his. It's a skill only God has. Remember when I said

I wanted to be a history teacher? Well, that wasn't too far off from the job God would lead me to. At all the corporate jobs I had had, I taught employees not just their job functions, but also how to think differently about the job and themselves.

As I became active in my church, I started to teach Sunday school. Now, I didn't *want* to teach Sunday school, but I did it anyway. One day, when a child asked a question I couldn't answer right away, I knew that I was right where God wanted me to be. It was so scary and yet so comforting, because I knew He hadn't to put me there to abandon me. Our best made plans will fail if they aren't God's ordained plans for our lives. We can try our best to fit them in, but it is so much easier to concede that God is in control.

Day 4

Today's C.H.A.N.G.E. Action:

Tear up your to-do-list. If you can't do that and need a list, take it, and whatever is first on that list, and cross it out. Replace it with this phrase: "Lord, show me what your plan is for me today."

_____

_____

_____

_____

_____

_____

_____

_____

_____

Reflection

DAY 5

Be Calm in the Middle of it All.

Mark 4:39
*"Then He arose and rebuked the wind,
and said to the sea, 'Peace, be still!' And the wind
ceased and there was a great calm."*

I am not much of a worrywart, but I have a really close sister friend who is. She worries about things that may or may not happen fifty years from now. She is an extremely proactive person, but she often makes plans without God's input. As I write this, I am reminded of Mary and Martha. If we were either of them, I would be Mary, not because I am such a great little Christian girl, but because I simply abhor cleaning house. My friend loves it, so I can see her all around the house making sure Jesus could lick her kitchen floor if He wanted to. One time, she called me in a panic about a decision one of her children was about to make. In that one choice, she had determined how the next five years of his life would be. I thought, we love our children so much that we don't want them to make the same mistakes we did, but if we don't allow them to get in a storm, how will they understand that Jesus can calm it?

The day I lost my job was one of the hardest of my life, yet I sat there cleaning out my desk with a sense of calm. It wasn't me, but it was the Holy Spirit working in me. This quiet confidence doesn't come automatically. You don't wake up one day and say, "I am filled with calmness." Your calmness comes from Jesus, whom you spend time with and have come to know all about it. You have been tested, and through those tests, you are reassured that He will bring peace and calm to your situation.

Day 5

Today's C.H.A.N.G.E. Action:

When you feel yourself growing worried, go to the scriptures. Pray. If you have to pray 100 times because you feel worrisome and anxious, pray 100 times.

_____

_____

_____

_____

_____

_____

_____

_____

_____

Reflection

_____

_____

_____

_____

_____

_____

_____

_____

_____

_____

_____

_____

_____

Humility produces honesty which allows us to give God honor. As we place God in His rightful place we can hear his spirit that brings hope.

"A change in behavior begins with a change in the heart." - **Unknown**

DAY 6

Humble Yourself Before the Lord

James 4:10
"Humble yourselves in the sight of the Lord, and He will lift you up."

C.S. Lewis said, "Humility is not thinking less of yourself, but thinking of yourself less." When we think too highly of ourselves, it becomes harder to submit to anyone in authority, let alone God, who is above all things. I thought I was a humble person for years because I was nice. But often in my words I was sarcastic, thinking it was funny, and I unknowingly would hurt people with my speech. When you do things and take on projects to get recognized, that does nothing for God. God searches the heart, and scripture says the heart is deceitful. The heart is has to fight to keep it sacred for God to dwell there. When we think of the things that hold us back, such as pride, selfishness, arrogance, and a lack of forgiveness, all are found in the deep recesses of our hearts. The opposites of those traits, humility, selflessness, and forgiveness, fight for position. We must constantly check our hearts. .

The truth is we think we are doing things for the good of others, but if we aren't careful, we can be guided by selfish intentions. Being humble means accepting that it was only through God's grace and mercy that we can come to the throne and allow our sins to be forgiven.

It's easy for some of us who have been delivered from something great like drug addiction or sexual promiscuity, or who have committed a heinous act and then found oue sins forgiven through the blood of Christ. But, for those of us who abide by society's standards of what is good, or don't have a troubling moment in our story of coming to Christ, humility might take a little more work. I recall a time when we were doing a dramatization of the seven stations of Christ for a Maundy Thursday service. My pastor told me I would be reciting the words of Mary Magdalene because she was always so thankful and I am always thanking God in my prayers. I honestly didn't realize how much I gave God thanks in my prayers. But, when I thought about all I have done, thought, or said, I couldn't help but think, "This man, this Jesus, my friend, loved *me* before I even loved myself to give up his life." And I am forever humbled by His love.

Day 6

Today's C.H.A.N.G.E. Action:

Think of yourself less today. Do three things for three different people today, one being someone you don't know. Pay for someone's meal behind you. Call someone on your church prayer list or send him or her a card. Do not expect anything in return, and do not tell anyone what you did.

_____

_____

_____

_____

_____

_____

_____

_____

Reflection

DAY 7

Hope is Built on Jesus

Psalm 147:11
*"But the Lord takes pleasure in those who fear him,
in those who hope in his steadfast love."*

Some of us wish, others hope. In my twenties I wished for everything. I was searching for luck. I had good luck shoes, and I had a good luck suit for interviews. I would read my horoscope and get my lucky numbers and be good to go! But, more often than not, my luck would run out, and my wishes never panned out. By the time I left my twenties and entered my thirties, I began to look at hope a little differently.

My grandfather Raymond would sing hymns like "My hope is built on nothing else than Jesus blood and righteousness." Hope is confident expectation. It is the knowledge that if we put everything in God's hands, He will do whatever He said he would do. Hope is walking around praising God when everything around you seems so uncertain and unclear, but you are confident in what tomorrow brings. Submission is difficult for us because we lose a sense of control, but hope helps remain confident in releasing control to God. Hope produces, love, and peace. We need hope to complete the Christian journey.

Day 7

Today's C.H.A.N.G.E. Action:

Think about something in your life right now that isn't going as expected but you are hoping changes. Pray for a change in that situation.

_____

_____

_____

_____

_____

_____

_____

_____

_____

Reflection

DAY 8

Hearing God's Voice

Romans 10:17
*"So faith comes from hearing, and hearing
through the word of Christ."*

Wondering if I am hearing God's voice or my own has
been one of the hardest things in my Christian journey.
Is God telling me to go this way, to do this, to start this
ministry, or to even write this book? There are times
when I have been jealous of others who say they have
heard God speak to them. I would sit there feeling
empty because I didn't hear God speak to me. Since I
didn't hear him speak to me, then he must not care
about how I am feeling. These are the feelings that I
would let take over my thought pattern. But I was
completely off. God speaks to all who speaks to him,
and even those who don't think they are speaking to
God.

We often refer to the Holy Spirit as "something." We say things such as, "Something told me to do this." It's okay to call it what it is—the Holy Spirit. The Holy Spirit is God's voice. We all have a personal relationship with Christ, so the unique way God gets my attention may differ from yours. Once we have completed our prayers and petitions, we have to listen to God's direction. We have to saturate what we hear with God's words from scripture.

Day 8

Today's C.H.A.N.G.E. Action:

Spend today in God's word through preaching, reading, or singing.

_____

_____

_____

_____

_____

_____

_____

_____

_____

_____

Reflection

DAY 9

Honesty

Psalm 101:7
*"No one who practices deceit shall dwell in my house;
no one who utters lies shall continue before my eyes."*

The little white lie is still a lie. It's funny that we don't think about it as such. Who among us calls out sick from work but isn't really sick? Me. I can recall an instance when I was called to do something at church that I didn't want to do it, and I didn't have a reason to not do it other than pure selfishness. I wanted to make something up. I wanted to lie. But the spirit convicts, and I couldn't lie. Lies separate us from God and our right place in the kingdom of God. Before you call out others for deceitful things, look at yourself and be honest with the person you are, and know that no matter your flaws, you are loved, you are free, and you are redeemed through the blood.

Day 9

Today's C.H.A.N.G.E. Action:

If I can't speak honestly, I will say nothing.

_____

_____

_____

_____

_____

_____

_____

_____

_____

_____

Reflection

_____

_____

_____

_____

_____

_____

_____

_____

_____

_____

_____

_____

_____

DAY 10

Give God Honor with our Hearts

Isaiah 29:13
"Therefore the Lord said: 'In as much as these people draw near with their mouths and honor Me with their lips, But have removed their hearts far from Me.'"

This is a personal relationship transformation and a constant reminder that Jesus is simply after your heart. Once you align your heart with the attributes of Christ, submission will come naturally. We make it so hard for ourselves because we think it's a chore, but it's only a chore when we allow barriers to block us from our relationship.

Honor begins in our hearts and the things we hold valuable. Your heart has to align with what your lips say. The mouth speaks what the heart is filled of, and it is important that you honor God with not just your lips but also your heart.

Day 10

Today's C.H.A.N.G.E. Action:

Search your heart to find anything that is not honoring God. Ask God to reveal it and remove it.

_____

_____

_____

_____

_____

_____

_____

_____

_____

_____

Reflection

_____

_____

_____

_____

_____

_____

_____

_____

_____

_____

_____

_____

_____

Accept the plan God has for our lives. He is awesome! If we abide in him we will begin to see His work within us.

"Progress is impossible without change & those who cannot change their minds cannot change anything"
- George Bernard Shaw

DAY 11

Accept the Plans God Has for You

Jeremiah 29:11 NLT
*"For I know the plans I have for you,' says the Lord.
'They are plans for good and not for disaster, to give you
a future and a hope."*

Maybe you don't know what to do with your life or where to go next. Well, guess what? God already has a plan. I always made plans for my life, but they didn't necessarily include God's plan. It wasn't until my wants aligned with His will that things start to sync. Once you can accept the will of God and believe that His plans are for your good, then you can walk in confidence knowing that God is going to give you a hope and a future.

When I lost my job after twelve years, I found myself starting over. It had been over a decade that I had to look for a job, and just that process had changed drastically. When I did get back into the work force I took a job that on paper appeared to be out of my comfort zone. In fact, it was opposite of everything I thought I would be able to do. I am not technical; I would categorize myself as a creative. Yet, I was given this opportunity to step out my comfort zone and learn something different. For a year and a half I learned about integrations and HTML coding, and as much as I didn't want to be technical, I was renewing my mind into understanding technical jargon. As prepared to be an independent author, I found myself having to build my own websites, integrate code, and build web applications.

God had a plan. He was preparing me all along for this journey, and had I stayed at the comfortable and familiar job of twelve plus years, I wouldn't have been taken out of the familiar in order to get the wisdom and knowledge to learn what I needed.

Day 11

Today's C.H.A.N.G.E. Action:

Think about what you have declined because you were fearful or didn't think you had the skills to do it. Pray on those things; it may be just part of God's plan for you. If you keep pulling away from something that you know you are supposed to do, accept the plan. Get in alignment with your assignment.

_____

_____

_____

_____

_____

_____

_____

_____

Reflection

_____

_____

_____

_____

_____

_____

_____

_____

_____

_____

_____

_____

_____

_____

DAY 12

Be Slow to Anger

James 1:19
"You must all be quick to listen, slow to speak, and slow to get angry."

Anger is a reaction of fear. Fear is a spirit not of God. We cannot let others dictate whether we get angry. Recently, I had to use this scripture to help me in my relationships, especially my marriage. I get angry quickly. I get angry over misinterpretations, mixed messages, and misunderstandings. My anger comes from a fear of not being appreciated or not being understood. So, I spent thirty days simply listening to God to get my heart right and in a position to speak what God wants me to say and not always what I want to say. Sometimes the things I want to say are mean spirited, hateful, condescending, and downright mean. When we get angry, we aren't showing others Jesus.

It's Time to Make a Change

Anger condemns, but love convicts. We want to look at others the way that God sees them.

Day 12

Today's C.H.A.N.G.E. Action:

Every time you feel yourself getting angry with someone, say "Jesus loves." That's it. Repeat it as many times as needed. Don't say anything else. Do not try to defend your position, debate your point, or justify your actions. Just say, out loud or silently, "Jesus loves."

_____

_____

_____

_____

_____

_____

_____

_____

_____

_____

Reflection

_____

_____

_____

_____

_____

_____

_____

_____

_____

_____

_____

_____

_____

DAY 13

God is Able

Ephesians 3:20
"Now to Him who is able to do exceedingly abundantly above all that we ask or think, according to the power that works in us."

You have to change your thought process so you will know and believe that God can do more than what you ask. I think the reason we so often fall short in our submission process is because we really can't fathom how incredible God is. He is able to do everything we need him to do. He is able to be everything we need him to be. He is able and capable of all things. This bears repeating, because we forget it when we are tired or think God isn't listening.

Day 13

Repeat this throughout the day: "GOD IS ABLE."

_____

_____

_____

_____

_____

_____

_____

_____

_____

_____

_____

Reflection

DAY 14

God is Awesome

Psalm 47:2
*"For the Lord Most High is awesome.
He is the great King of all the earth."*

God is awesome and worthy of our praise. We must always keep God in reverence and in a position of greatness. God is great and worthy of our praise all the time. The Book of Psalms is where many of the songs we sing are derived. In God's divinity, He can fix anything that we struggle with. In His humanity, He can identify anything we are struggling with, which makes Him awesome.

There simply are no words to express how great God is. The longer you walk with Christ, the more you begin to see how awesome He is.

Day 14

Today's C.H.A.N.G.E. Action:

Read Psalm 47:1-6

_____

_____

_____

_____

_____

_____

_____

_____

_____

_____

_____

Reflection

DAY 15

Abide in Him

John 15:4
"Abide in Me, and I in you. As the branch cannot bear fruit of itself, unless it abides in the vine, neither can you, unless you abide in Me."

We are at our greatest when we stay connected to Christ. We cannot do anything without him. No matter what happens, we must remain connected to the vine. First, Jesus uses this metaphor to teach us that He and God are one. Second, the vine is the source of life for believers. We have to consistently remain close to Jesus.

Abiding in him through our prayers and our service to others, everything we do should be with Him. When we try to do things without Him, we fall short.

Day 15

What are you doing to bear fruit? What are you not doing?

_____

_____

_____

_____

_____

_____

_____

_____

_____

73

Reflection

Stop being **Negative**. There are so many areas we find ourselves being negative, from the people we call friends, our own self destructive thoughts, negative about our job, and actions. This should be the first thing we do to change.

"Close some doors. Not because of pride, incapacity or arrogance, but simply because they no longer lead somewhere" - **Unknown**

DAY 16

Neutralize Negative People and Thoughts

Philippians 4:8 GW
*"Finally, brothers and sisters, keep your thoughts
on whatever is right or deserves praise: things
that are true, honorable, fair, pure, acceptable,
or commendable."*

Neutralize negative people, things, and thoughts.
Negativity is a tool the adversary uses to distract us
from our goals and our callings. Remove anything that
is causing you bitterness, and anything that isn't from
God. When Paul wrote this letter to the church at
Philippi, he was in prison. He was encouraging these
congregations of believers to live, eat, think, and
breathe Christ. It was essential during times of
adversity and anxiety to remember to rejoice and see
the joy in everything. And we must do the same. God

inhabits the praise of His people, and when we start praising and honoring God, He will react, and those negative thoughts and negative people will quickly disappear.

Day 16

Today's C.H.A.N.G.E. Action:

Do not say one negative thing today. If someone around you says anything negative, do not acknowledge it. Instead, change the subject or change your environment.

_____

_____

_____

_____

_____

_____

_____

_____

_____

Reflection

_____

_____

_____

_____

_____

_____

_____

_____

_____

_____

_____

_____

DAY 17

Neutralize Negative Thoughts about Yourself

Psalm 139:14
"I will praise You, for I am fearfully and wonderfully made."

Many times in my life I didn't think I was good enough to do something. Fear of failing holds us back from accomplishing goals and moving forward. You have to fight through those thoughts and realize that you are God's creation. If He is sovereign, and He is the Creator of all things, then we must know that He created something special. When it comes to scriptures, the intent is to fully understand the complexity of the human body.

Our brains have the ability to learn, think, react, and control how we walk and talk in conjunction with doing other things. Realizing that this body was created in such a careful and exact way releases the negative thoughts we think of about ourselves.

Day 17

Today's C.H.A.N.G.E. Action:

When you are having negative thoughts about yourself, recite Psalm 139:14.

_____

_____

_____

_____

_____

_____

_____

_____

_____

_____

Reflection

DAY 18

Neutralize Negative Thoughts about Your Job

Colossians 3:23
"Work willingly at whatever you do, as though you were working for the Lord rather than for people."

Often, I find myself repeating this verse. I have been fortunate that for most of my adult life I have had jobs that I love. More recently, I have been tested at jobs that I knew weren't going to give me any fulfillment except a paycheck. Sometimes we are placed in situations to teach us. I was at a job that took me completely out of my comfort zone but prepared me for starting my own business. It is easy to say that if you don't like your job, leave. Of course, sometimes it is not that easy. Truthfully, if you absolutely cannot find one good thing about your job, then you should ask yourself why you are there. Some of us get complacent in situations, and then, rather than trusting and seeking God's counsel, we get bitter and complain.

If you have a negative approach to your job, whether in the form of complaint or lackadaisical work ethic, and you do not put forth effort, remember that through your actions you are honoring God and showing your co-workers Jesus through. You cannot take your job for granted.

Day 18

Today's C.H.A.N.G.E. Action:

Find something positive about your job and meditate on that today.

_____

_____

_____

_____

_____

_____

_____

_____

_____

_____

_____

Reflection

DAY 19

Neutralize Negative Speech

Ephesians 4:29
"Don't say anything that would hurt another person. Instead, speak only what is good so that you can give help wherever it is needed. That way, what you say will help those who hear you."

Words have power. When we speak positively and with authority, we have the power to activate a change in the atmosphere. When we speak the word of God over a situation, something shifts. I use this verse a lot when teaching my children to speak nicely around each other. When we speak what is good, we are showing people Jesus through our words. We are speaking life, and not death, into a situation.

The tongue is very powerful, and we have to guard our speech with goodness.

Day 19

Today's C.H.A.N.G.E. Action:

If you cannot say anything good, remain silent. Tell three people something good or helpful.

_____

_____

_____

_____

_____

_____

_____

_____

_____

_____

It's Time to Make a Change

Reflection

_____

_____

_____

_____

_____

_____

_____

_____

_____

_____

_____

_____

_____

DAY 20

Neutralize Negative Actions

James 1:22
"Do not merely listen to the world, and so deceive yourselves. Do what it says."

All of us find ways to self-destruct. We use drugs, drink alcohol, have sex, eat too much food, gamble, or shop too much. I spent years in depression over failed goals and relationships, and by the time I was thirty, I had a failed marriage, two children with different fathers, a criminal record, and a shopping addiction. I didn't even realize I was an emotional shopper for many years. When I would find myself having a bad day, I found myself with a new purse, too. Of course, the purse would need a nice pair of shoes to go with it. It was a repetitive cycle that I couldn't break. It would be fifteen years of this destructive behavior before I realized I had a problem. I was able to feed this need for things because I had always had someone to help me with bills. When I became the sole provider for my family, that all changed. Now that I couldn't spend money on frivolous items, I became resentful because my husband was out of work. Self-destruction was my middle name.

It would be easy to blame all these things on the devil, but why should I give him all this credit? I played a starring role in my life and was responsible for the way it had turned out. When I finally broke free from all the guilt and shame of my sins, I was able to see that God loved me. He cared so much about me that He died for me. He wanted the best for me. He thinks I am good, so He took this broken vessel and molded it back together for His glory. God wants the best for you as well. He wants to take every hurt, every sin, and every piece of you and mold it back together for His goodness. He is a merciful God.

Day 20

Know that you are redeemed and made good in God's eyes. Any negative behavior you had, it is erased.

_____

_____

_____

_____

_____

_____

_____

_____

_____

_____

_____

Reflection

_____

_____

_____

_____

_____

_____

_____

_____

_____

_____

_____

_____

_____

_____

Give. It is a small little four letter word with so much power, but love and giving go together. John 3:16 tells us that God so loved the world, that he sacrificed--he GAVE his only son. Give thanks, give yourself, give love, Give, and then recognize the gift that God has left us with. And then Go! Go out and give!

"Be the change you want to see in the world"
- Mohandas Gandhi

DAY 21

Give Thanks

Thessalonians 5:18
"Whatever happens, give thanks, because it is God's will in Christ Jesus that you do this."

When we can be thankful in all circumstances, we see God being active in our lives. Gratitude makes it easier to submit because we realize that there is a lot we have to be thankful for. Whatever season you are in on your way to success, you must live in that moment. Even if you tried something new and it failed. Being thankful just for the opportunity keeps you from becoming fearful to try again. Your attitude should be to have gratitude in all things.

I look back on when my job closed without notice. While it was the most unfortunate time in my life, I am thankful for it. Losing my job helped me to put God in the right place.

Day 21

Today's C.H.A.N.G.E. Action:

Find three things that may have caused an inconvenience and thank God for them. It could be traffic on your way to work, a cake that fell, or an argument with a loved one. Find the teaching moment.

_____

_____

_____

_____

_____

_____

_____

_____

_____

Reflection

_____

_____

_____

_____

_____

_____

_____

_____

_____

_____

_____

_____

_____

DAY 22

Give Yourself to God

Romans 12:1
"Brothers and sisters, in view of all we have just shared about God's compassion, I encourage you to offer your bodies as living sacrifices, dedicated to God and pleasing to him. This kind of worship is appropriate for you."

Being always available for God gives Him joy. He gave you all these wonderful gifts and attributes, some you recognize and some you hide. Still, He is waiting for you to share them not just with others, but also with Him. He wants you to give them back to Him as gratitude. He created you for His glory, and that should stick with you always. This is never about you and always about Him.

Day 22

Today's C.H.A.N.G.E. Action:

What are you doing with your talents that you can give thanks to God?

_____

_____

_____

_____

_____

_____

_____

_____

_____

_____

_____

Reflection

_____

_____

_____

_____

_____

_____

_____

_____

_____

_____

_____

_____

_____

DAY 23

Be a Generous Giver

Luke 6:38

"Give, and you will receive. Your gift will return to you in full—pressed down, shaken together to make room for more, running over, and poured into your lap. The amount you give will determine the amount you get back."

The Gospel of Luke, which is where this verse comes from, has an underlying message of Jesus' compassion to mankind. We see Jesus as the Son of Man, and He can empathize with us. In the preceding verse, Jesus is teaching us not to judge others, to not condemn others, and to always forgive others. And then he says, "Give and you will receive." Many interpret this to mean monetary giving, and that's fine, but giving doesn't just start and stop at money. We can give our time, gifts, service, love, peace, patience, and anything that you have been blessed with you give back. God blesses us with so many things, and we have to give back.

In biblical times, there were less Christians in need because there was a spirit of sharing and giving. However, there was a couple in the Book of Acts (Acts 5:1-11) who sold their land, and instead of giving Peter and the disciples the full amount, they gave a portion and lied about what they had received. When we feel we have to hide our gifts and our treasures from God, we miss blessings. Sharing and giving is the essence of being a Christian.

God so loved the world that He *gave* His only son, and giving is what God does over and over. Everything comes from God. You can't beat God's blessings in your life.

Day 23

Today's C.H.A.N.G.E. Action:

What are you holding back from God and from others?
Start giving today.

_____

_____

_____

_____

_____

_____

_____

_____

_____

_____

Reflection

_____

_____

_____

_____

_____

_____

_____

_____

_____

_____

_____

_____

DAY 24

Recognize the Gift

John 14:27
*"I am leaving you with a gift--peace of mind and heart.
And the peace I give is a gift the world cannot give.
So don't be troubled or afraid."*

The sacrifice of Jesus' life for our atonement is shown with the gifts He left us. In this case, the gift is peace, but there are many, many more. There is the gift of grace and mercy, the gift of justification by faith, the Holy Spirit, access to the Father, reconciliation to God, and the list continues. We have to recognize the gift and give thanks. Understanding the gift of grace, for instance, allows us to be gracious to others. By the grace of God, I am here today writing this book, using my gifts, and sharing my mess. I didn't earn anything, and I don't deserve it.

When we can look at our own situation and see grace bestowed over and over again, it allows us to be gracious to others. In God's eyes, we are perfect. He doesn't see any flaw, any blemish, or any wrong, because when God looks at us, He sees Jesus, his son. We have to look at others the same way that God looks at us. Recognize the gifts that have placed you in right standing with the Father Almighty.

Day 24

Today's C.H.A.N.G.E. Action:

Are you ignoring the gifts that Jesus has left? Take some time today and search the scriptures for those gifts and write them down. Thank God for them.

_____

_____

_____

_____

_____

_____

_____

_____

_____

_____

Reflection

DAY 25

Get Up and Go!

Matthew 28:19
*"Therefore, go and make disciples of all the nations,
baptizing them in the name of the Father and the Son
and the Holy Spirit"*

In the Bible, the word "go" appears 1,544 times. In order
to submit, we have to go when God tells us to. The great
commission requires us to "go and make disciples." We
can't do this by watching TV, idolizing things, being
bitter, or using hateful words and harsh tones. You have
to believe that God isn't going to take you anywhere or
have you do anything without Him. He has equipped
you to do anything he has asked. But first you have to
believe. You can't do anything on your own, but with
Christ you can do all things. God does not call on the
qualified—He qualifies the called. You were born for a
purpose, and you must believe that God wants the very
best for you.

Day 25

Think about what God has asked you to do that you haven't done. What is stopping you?

_____

_____

_____

_____

_____

_____

_____

_____

_____

_____

Reflection

Encourage each other in Christ. **Embrace** others with the love of God. Remember that He is everlasting and endures all things. But, most important. **Enjoy** the journey and always be willing to re-evaluate.

"Yesterday I was clever, so I wanted to change the world. Today I am wise so I am changing myself"
- Rumi

DAY 26

Endure

James 5:11
*"Indeed we count them blessed who endure.
You have heard of the perseverance of Job and seen the
end intended by the Lord—that the Lord is very
compassionate and merciful."*

This Christian journey is full of trials and tribulations, good and bad. When James, a stoic believer and leader of the early church, wrote this letter, Christians were being persecuted and many were questioning and doubting their faith. But James assured them that they had to fight for their faith and endure the challenges. If you, too, do this, you will be considered blessed. God sees all and knows all. Your labor is not in vain. Do not give up.

Day 26

Today's C.H.A.N.G.E. Action:

To those who are weary, take today to stay in the stillness of the Father. The joy of the Lord is your strength. Think about the Lord as you encounter your situation and seek His strength.

_____

_____

_____

_____

_____

_____

_____

_____

_____

Reflection

DAY 27

He Encourages

Matthew 11:28-29
*"Come to me, all who labor and are heavy laden,
and I will give you rest. Take my yoke upon you, and
learn from me, for I am gentle and lowly in heart,
and you will find rest for your souls."*

Submitting to God may seem like a lot of work, and at times it is. After all, we wear many hats in our lives, and it can be difficult to juggle everything and maintain balance. Anytime you feel like you can't go on, he will give you rest. Scripture after scripture reminds us that we can find solace and rest in His loving arm. He isn't going to leave us. Even when we leave him, He is so faithful that He forgives us and continues to provide for us.

Day 27

Today's C.H.A.N.G.E. Action:

Because God encourages us with scripture and promises, encourage someone today. Find someone who is heavy laden, and speak to him or her with encouraging words.

_____

_____

_____

_____

_____

_____

_____

_____

Reflection

_____

_____

_____

_____

_____

_____

_____

_____

_____

_____

_____

_____

_____

DAY 28

He is Everlasting

1 John 2:25
*"And in this fellowship we enjoy the eternal life
he promised us."*

Submitting to God isn't really about this world. It is about solidifying the fellowship so we can enjoy eternal life with God. Christ died for us and endured a brutal and horrifying death for us, yet we still don't fully trust in Him. We fall short every day to honor Him with everything we have. When we submit, we fully anticipate the eternal life that is promised.

Day 28

Today's C.H.A.N.G.E. Action:

Memorize this scripture and think about what it means to you.

_____

_____

_____

_____

_____

_____

_____

_____

_____

_____

Reflection

_____

_____

_____

_____

_____

_____

_____

_____

_____

_____

_____

_____

_____

DAY 29

Embrace Others

1 Thessalonians 5:11
"Therefore comfort each other and edify one another, just as you also are doing."

Part of a well-balanced Christian life is to be with other believers. I am a strong believer of surrounding yourself with other Christians and people whom love you. We aren't made to be alone, and we can't live this life alone. We are called to be in fellowship one with one another. Embrace others who can help you and hold you accountable. When you are having a bad day, they will love you and nurture you.

Day 29

Become active in a ministry. If you are already active, seek out someone that may be struggling in her faith and encourage her.

Reflection

DAY 30

Enjoy the Journey

Luke 1:47
"And my spirit rejoices in God my Savior"

This Christian life is a fulfilling life. We can look at nature and the way God uses nature to teach us, and we can look at every small, intimate detail of a situation and how God uses it to show us He is God. We see beauty in ugliness because our perception is transformed, and we can see Jesus working on our behalf. Then, we get it! When you submit to God, you experience life in this fascinating way, just like Elizabeth and Mary did when they connected and "got each other."

Don't think of submission as losing something. You are gaining so much more. Enjoy the journey that you are on and know that you are not alone. You have been chosen. You are redeemed by the blood of Jesus. You are loved. You are free.

Day 30

Today's C.H.A.N.G.E. Action:

Think about a situation you may have overlooked at first, but after much thought, realized was a God moment.

_____

_____

_____

_____

_____

_____

_____

_____

_____

Reflection

_____

_____

_____

_____

_____

_____

_____

_____

_____

_____

_____

_____

_____

about shani mcilwain

Shani McIlwain was born in Los Angeles in the Queen of Angels Hospital. In 1982, she and her mother moved to Hancock, New York. While there, she learned to play the violin, played sports, studied scripture, and adopted her love her writing. After high school, she went to Hampton University where she majored in History Education.

From college, she moved to DC, delivered her son, got married, had a daughter, and then divorced. Not long after, she lost her mother, birthed another daughter, and then twin girls, one of whom passed away. She later remarried, found work as a Quality and Business Process Manager, joined a church, and began her journey of healing through spirituality, love and writing.

In the middle of her mess, she realized that Jesus is real. "He's more than a song. He's bigger than anything and everything I could imagine, and I wholeheartedly believe that my calling is to empower others to get know Jesus in a way that will transform their lives."

She enjoys writing, teaching, storytelling, speaking, giving back to the community, spending time with her family, and having fun! For more information, be sure to visit www.ShanimcIlwain.com.

WE WANT TO HEAR FROM YOU!!!

If this book has made a difference in your life
Shani would be delighted to hear about it.

Leave a review on Amazon.com!

BOOK SHANI TO SPEAK AT YOUR NEXT EVENT!

Send an email to booking@publishyourgift.com

Learn more about Shani at
www.ShaniMcIlwain.com

FOLLOW SHANI ON SOCIAL MEDIA

  SharingMyMess ShaniMcIlwain
